HELP: I'VE BEEN ADOPTED!

Brenda McCreight, PH.D., R.S.W.

Help: I've Been Adopted
By Brenda McCreight, Ph.D., R.S.W.
Published through Tapestry Books

Interior Book Design and Layout by
www.integrativeink.com

ISBN: 978-0-9843684-0-2

TABLE OF CONTENTS

FOREWORD

Why I Wrote This Book

I work with lots of children and teens who have been adopted and it's not uncommon for them to have problems adjusting to their new lives. I help them express their questions about their life changes when they are in my office, but I've often wished I could give them a book that presented the problems and provided some solutions so that they could read it at home when they are in the mood. This book was written so that YOU can learn about some of the issues that are common in the lives of people who have been adopted, and to help you find ways to communicate your feelings to your new parents.

I also wrote this book for adoptive parents and adoption professionals who want to have a more neutral way to bring up topics that might be difficult to present to their child or client.

INTRODUCTION

How This Book Can Help You

Congratulations! It's finally happened. You have been adopted.

Perhaps you've been waiting and hoping you would be adopted for a long time...

Or maybe you only recently found out that you could be adopted and this was a surprise to you...

Maybe you're mad about being adopted because you secretly hoped that your birth parents were going to take you home...

There are so many different feelings that run through the minds of children and teens when they get adopted that the process can be overwhelming.

The parents who have adopted you are also going through some changes now that you have joined their lives. Maybe you are the first child or teen that your new parents have ever adopted. Or, maybe you are the fifteenth to come into their family. But, no matter what you thought or hoped for in your new adoptive family, no matter what type of family you came from, and no matter what type of family you have been adopted into, you will find that things are not quite what you expected!

You may have been hoping for a rich family, maybe even a movie star family, but instead you got a family that works hard on a farm. Or, maybe you wanted to be someone's only child, but you ended up being placed in a family where you have four new older siblings and two new younger siblings. Or, maybe you never had any particular hopes about adoption at all. You might have been afraid to wish for something because most of the time the things you wish for don't come true. But, I'm sure you had some kind of thoughts about being adopted, and in this book we're going to explore the common feelings that kids and teens experience when the adoption event finally happens. This book will help you to understand that you are not alone with your questions. You can also use it to help your new family understand some of the emotions that you are feeling, but can't quite find the right words to express. This book includes suggestions to help you with the adjustment, but don't worry if some of them won't work for your situation. Give them a try! You've come this far, why not try to go just a bit farther...Good luck!

CHAPTER ONE

Hopes and Dreams about Being Adopted

Some kids who are adopted think that all of their problems are going to go away now that they have a new family. They believe that once they have parents they won't lie anymore, or steal, or set fires, or continue doing the kinds of behaviors that have always gotten them into trouble. They hope that their grades will go up, and that they will make a million new friends in their new school, even though they've never had good grades and have never been able to make friends before.

Often, kids who are getting adopted think that their adoptive parents will never get mad at them, no matter what they do, and that kids will never feel anger toward their adoptive parents. Many children believe that their adoptive parents are going to be perfect, and they are very surprised and even disappointed when they find out that the adoptive parents make mistakes, and don't always listen carefully or understand everything.

There are children and teens who didn't want to get adopted, and who are mad that they didn't have a choice about the matter. They told their social workers that they didn't want a new family but the social worker placed them with one anyway, and they feel angry even before they get to know their new parents. These kids often feel that they still belong with their birth parents, and they are afraid that now they are adopted, their birth parents will think they don't love them anymore.

There are also kids or teens who have waited a long time for a family, and who are very happy about being adopted. They like the new parents and they like the new life, but even happy children can have problems adjusting to the new home, the new parents, the new siblings, the new bedroom, the new clothes, the new school, and the new friends. Getting adopted isn't just about getting permanent parents; adoption changes everything in the adoptees' life.

Confusing Feelings

Regardless of how you feel about being adopted, it can still be a confusing and lonely time. No matter how many other families you've had, you will still not be fully prepared for all the feelings that arise after the adoption. That is because once the adoption takes place, you are having the one experience you never had before: *you are now living with parents who chose you, who can afford you, who can protect you, who will raise you, who will try hard to do what is right for you, who will teach you what is right and wrong, who will see to it that get a good education, who will teach you how to behave, and who will love you for the rest of your life.*

When something is this new and this big, it can make you feel like your whole world has turned upside down inside out. You might find that your thoughts are swirling around faster than you can control, so nothing comes out making sense. Or, you might find that suddenly all of your feelings have disappeared and you are left numb inside. Some kids get nervous and twitchy, while others get angry.

You might find that you want to talk about this, but you're afraid to say anything in case you say it wrong, or in case people think you are stupid. You might be afraid to tell your new parents how strange you are feeling because you don't want to hurt their feelings or make them mad. You might be trying to tell them all of your feelings, but it just comes out in a jumbled rage.

All of these feelings are normal. Most children or teens who get adopted are confused and unsettled--you are no different than the millions of other adopted children and adolescents in the world.

Up for Discussion: *What I Wanted*

Here are some 'I' statements you might want to discuss with your parents or your counselor. Some of them will apply to you, some won't. Just work on the statements that are right for your life:

- I wanted to be adopted because...

- I didn't want to be adopted because...

- I hoped my new family would be...

- I didn't want my new family to...

- I wanted to stay in touch with my foster family because...

- I didn't want to stay in touch with my foster family because...

- I wanted to stay in touch with my birth family because...

- I didn't want to stay in touch with my birth family because...

- I wanted to stay with my birth siblings because...

- I didn't want to stay with my birth siblings because...

- I was afraid of what my new adoptive parents would be like because...

- I would feel happier if my new parents would...

- Here is what I could do to help with our family's changes and adjustments...

Jimmy's Story

Jimmy, age ten, never thought much about being adopted. He had been in the same foster home for a long time and no one ever talked to him or to his two younger sisters about having another family. He liked his foster parents, but they were kind of old and sometimes they wouldn't let him do things that other kids could do, like have overnights or join soccer, but otherwise Jimmy thought his life was fine.

There were some aspects of his life that Jimmy really liked, even though he felt guilty. Whenever he lied or stole, Jimmy would blame it on his sisters and his foster parents always believed him. He hardly ever got in trouble, even though he deserved to, and his sisters weren't so lucky.

One day, a new social worker came to their house and told Jimmy and his sisters that they were going to be adopted soon. A forever family had been found for them and they would begin visiting, and then move to their new home, by the end of the school year.

That was a real shock for Jimmy. The social worker told him what was special about having a 'forever' family, but Jimmy didn't really understand--he just said he did so that he could stop talking to her. His sisters were really excited about the adoption, but they were always excited about everything so he couldn't talk to them about it.

Jimmy and his sisters met the new parents on a Saturday afternoon and they began to have visits every weekend. The new parents were nice, and they did fun activities that the foster parents never did with the kids. They also had a huge house with lots of outdoor play equipment in the back yard. The bedrooms that were going to be his and his sisters' had lots of room and big closets for all the new toys Jimmy thought his new parents would buy for him.

Jimmy and his sisters moved in with their forever parents, but after a few weeks, Jimmy began to think that maybe this adoption wasn't going to be so good after all. His new parents spent time with the kids and they let him join soccer, which he liked. However, they didn't keep buying him stuff, and they also didn't believe him when he blamed his sisters for what he did. They talked about him being a liar and often took away his privileges. In fact, it seemed like these people were kind of mean! Jimmy also wasn't very happy with the rules. He thought a forever family would let him do more of what he wanted, but instead they had more rules than his foster parents.

Jimmy was starting to feel kind of angry toward these forever people. The whole adoption experience wasn't turning out to be the way he thought it would.

Jimmy's Solution

What do you think Jimmy could do to help fix this? How could Jimmy's parents help fix this? If you have these types of feelings, here are some suggestions for you and your family to try:

- **Tell your parents how you are feeling.**

- **Listen to the reasons your parents give you for why they have the new rules.** If you don't understand what they mean, let them know. Don't be afraid to say "*I don't understand*".

- **If you don't like their reasons, tell them in a polite way.** Offer to problem-solve and compromise.

- **Can't get everything you want?** Ask your parents and your counselor to help you learn to cope with some of the changes and the new rules.

One day Jimmy got so fed up with the rules that he phoned his social worker and asked to be moved. After all, that was what always happened before in his life. He was very surprised when his social worker said he couldn't be moved just because he didn't like the rules, as this was where he was going to spend the rest of his growing up years.

Jimmy's parents knew he was unhappy so they decided that the whole family would go to counseling to learn how to live together. The counselor saw all the kids and the parents together and the first thing she did was to help them learn how to talk to each other in a way that didn't involve yelling. That was really new and helpful to Jimmy, even though it was hard for him to do. Then, she began to work on how the family decided on rules. It turned out that his parents weren't going to change all of the rules, but they were willing to get rid of a few, and that made Jimmy happier. Jimmy also had to learn how to accept responsibility and not blame his sisters for every bad thing he did. That was really difficult for Jimmy, but the counselor helped his parents learn to speak to Jimmy in a way that didn't make him so upset when he was caught lying or misbehaving.

Life got better after that, and Jimmy has now lived with his family for two years. Sometimes he still feels frustrated, but he uses his words to tell his parents and they talk about the problem. Jimmy doesn't want to move anymore.

CHAPTER TWO

Why Do Kids Get Adopted?

All kinds of kids and teens get adopted. It is never, ever is because of something the child did wrong, or because he or she wasn't good enough or pretty enough or smart enough, or the right color or the right height *or the right or wrong anything*! Adoption happens because the birth parents had so many problems that their child ended up needing a new family.

Here are some of the common reasons that a child or teen might be placed for adoption:

The birth parents were too young to take care of the child. This happens when birth parents have a baby while they are too young to earn the money to buy a baby food or clothes, or to afford a place to live. There isn't any particular age when birth parents are 'old enough' to take care of a baby; it's different in every situation.

The birth mother was single and already had a child or children, and couldn't manage to take care of any more. The birth mom may have wanted to keep her child, but if she had severe financial or housing problems, or emotional stress, it would have been too difficult for her to have one more baby to manage. She had to make a choice between keeping the baby but never being able to give the child a good life, or placing the baby with adoptive parents who could give the baby the life she felt her son or daughter deserved.

The birth parents had problems with addiction (drugs, alcohol, gambling, or the internet, for example). This is a very common reason for kids to need a new family. The birth parents get addicted to substances that take all of their time, energy, money and attention, which makes it impossible for them to take care of a child--or even care for themselves.

The birth parents were mentally or physically abusive to the child. This can happen because the birth parents took drugs or alcohol, or because they had a mental illness, or because they were emotionally unstable, or because they were beaten as a child and they never recovered from the emotional problems that resulted. Whatever the reason, they hurt their child, and that is against the law and can't be allowed to continue.

There was ongoing violence between the birth parents. In some families, the birth parents are violent. It can be that the birth dad beats the birth mom, or, if the birth dad is not with her, perhaps the birth mom has boyfriends who beat her. Sometimes it is the mom who is violent, or a relative who lives with the family. Even if the child isn't hit, he or she can become emotionally damaged from witnessing the violence, and needs to be removed from the situation.

The birth parents sexually abused the child, or didn't protect the child when others sexually abused him or her. No one is quite sure why people would ever do this to a child or teen, or why a parent would let another person abuse a child, but when it happens, it must be stopped and the child has to be protected. There can't be any second chances because we know that people who sexually abuse children don't stop just because they have been caught.

The birth parents live in a country where there is war or poverty and could not get enough food or medicine for the child. There are wars and extreme poverty in countries all over the world. It doesn't matter if the birth parents were kind or mean, they still might not have been able to find food for their children, so parents place them in orphanages where they can be fed, cared for and, hopefully, adopted by someone who lives in a safer part of the world.

The birth parents died. Sometimes birth parents die from accidents, disease, or war, and there is no one else in the family who can take care of the children.

The first adoptive parents were the wrong parents. Social workers try to place children into the best family they can find. But, on occasion, the child, the social worker and the parents begin to realize that something isn't working out and never will. For whatever reason, the adoptive parents are just not right for the child, and so a new adoptive family has to be found for the child or teen.

Even when a child knows the reasons why he had to be adopted, it might not make sense to him. He may still feel confused or angry about the situation and the decisions that led to adoption. Often, children or teens have to wait until they grow up before they can really come to terms with the reasons.

They may feel it isn't fair that they were adopted, and they are right--it isn't fair! Nothing about adoption is fair. But, adoption is what has to happen for a child or teen when he can't be raised by the birth parents. That is what happened to you.

Up for Discussion: *Understanding Why*

Questions you might want to think about...Some of them will apply to you, some won't. Just work on the questions that are right for your life:

- I lived with my birth parents for...

- Some of the problems my birth mother had were...

- Some of the problems my birth father had were...

- Some of the people who tried to help our family stay together were...

- Some of the places we lived were...

- Some of the people I knew when we lived together were...

- I couldn't stay with my birth parents because...

- (If you were adopted before and had to leave your adoptive family, you may apply the same questions to your adoption)

Lawanda's Story

Lawanda, age thirteen, lived with her birth parents until she was eight years old. It wasn't very much fun when she lived with them because they took drugs every weekend. The money her mom earned working at the restaurant during the week was spent on drugs instead of on food or rent. After her dad went to prison for a robbery, things got even worse. Sometimes Lawanda and her mom would move in the middle of the night because her mom couldn't pay the landlord. Those moves always scared Lawanda the most because she was afraid of the dark, and going out into the cold night was horrible.

Sometimes, Lawanda's mom had boyfriends who helped with the money, but sometimes the boyfriends spent more than her mom did.

By the time Lawanda was eight, her mom was stoned almost all of the time; the police and social workers kept coming to their apartment and taking Lawanda to foster care. Finally, her mom didn't get her back anymore. Lawanda wasn't sure if her mom had tried to get her back, or if her mom had just given up. After Lawanda's adoption, she never saw or heard from her mom, or her dad.

Her new parents were really nice people, and she was starting to feel pretty good about her new life. But Lawanda was afraid to trust that this was going to last. She asked her new parents about what had happened to her mom and dad, but they didn't have much information. To Lawanda, it seemed like lots of people had made lots of decisions about her life without ever keeping track of them all, and without ever telling her what was going on.

One day at school, a girl asked Lawanda how she got to be adopted. Lawanda just wanted to drop through the floor because she really didn't know. She didn't know who had made the decision to start the adoption process, or how the new parents had been found.

At night, Lawanda would lie in bed and worry about what was going to happen to her life. She wondered whether it was okay to really love her adoptive parents, or if someone would just decide she had to move again...

Lawanda's Solution

What do you think Lawanda could do to help fix this? What could Lawanda's adoptive parents do to help fix this? If you have these types of worries, here are some suggestions for you and your family to try:

- **Tell your adoptive parents that you would like to know more about why you couldn't stay with your birth parents.** Tell your adoptive parents that you would like to know if your mom and dad are okay, even if you can't have contact with them.

- **Ask your social worker if she can find out more information about your life and how the decisions were made that affected you.**

- **Ask your adoptive parents if they will do a Life Book for you** (your parents can easily buy a Life Book that they can fill in with whatever information they have about you and your birth family). Talk to your adoptive parents about what you should say when other people ask you nosey questions about your adoption

- **Ask your parents if it's possible that you could ever be moved again.** Ask your adoptive parents to explain why they believe they will never let you go.

- **Ask your adoptive parents how you have made their lives better.**

One night, Lawanda's adoptive mom found her crying in her room and she asked her what was wrong. Lawanda poured out all her worries. Her mom put her arms around her and held her for a long time, way after she had stopped crying. Then her mom called her dad into the room and explained all the things that Lawanda was worried about. The next day they made an appointment with the adoption worker to have her explain to Lawanda more about her adoption, and why it happened to her. They also promised that they would ask the social worker to find out if her birth parents were alright.

Lawanda still worries a bit because she knows that life can change even when people don't want it to, but when she gets upset, she tells her adoptive mom and they talk about it until she feels better.

CHAPTER THREE

Adoption and the Legal Process

Even the children and teens who have been adopted often don't know the process that occurred to get them from their birth parents to the adoptive parents. They know that social workers, and sometimes police, have been involved in their lives, and they know that judges have made decisions about where and with whom they can live. They know that they lived with one or more sets of foster parents, or in one or more treatment centers or group homes, or in one or more orphanages or on the street. Some have lived with relatives for awhile, maybe with a grandparent or an aunt. However, grown ups have a way of talking around children instead of *to* them, and so sometimes the children don't really understand the events and decisions that led to their being adopted.

Birth Parents

The one thing that that all adopted kids have in common is that they started life with their birth mother. The birth mom might have been young or old, nice or mean, pretty or ugly, alone or married, sober or drunk. She might have loved her child very much, or she might have had emotional problems that made it impossible for her to love anyone.

Some birth parents are able to take care of a baby, but their life style problems (mentioned in Chapter Two) are so big that other people in the community begin to realize that the baby or toddler is not safe. When that happens, they call the government social worker, whose job is to make sure that all children are safe and cared for.

Social Workers

The social worker is a person hired by the government or agency to protect children. When the government or agency receives a report that birth parents are not taking proper care of a child, they assign a social worker to investigate what the problems are, and whether the birth parents can improve their parenting skills.

In this country, once the social workers are involved, they help the birth parents get the right support or services to fix their problems. They offer counseling and parenting help, and treatment for addictions. But, if the birth parents can't change their lives enough to keep the child safe, then eventually the social worker must make the decision that the child can no longer wait for the parents' lives to improve, and presents the evidence, or reasons, why the birth parents can't raise the child to a judge.

Judges

Judges are trained to look at all of the evidence and decide if it is reasonable for birth parents to try again with more support, or if the birth parents have had enough chances to learn to keep their child safe. The judges listen to the evidence presented by the social workers, and if the birth parents don't agree that the child should be taken from them, he will also listen to what the birth parents have to say about how they live and how they can take care of the child. The judge also listens to anyone who has been trying to help the birth parents, such as counselors and doctors. Judges make sure that they have had all the evidence presented to them before the decision is made.

When the judge finally decides that the birth parents are not going to improve their ability to take care of their child, then he will end the birth parents' legal right to raise the child. This means that the child no longer belongs to the birth parents and can no longer live with them. Sometimes judges will let the child and the birth parents keep having visits, but sometimes the judges decide that the birth parents have too many problems to behave well around the child and so the judge won't let the birth parents have contact.

After this legal decision happens, it is then up to different social workers to find a new family for the child.

Alternate Care

In the meantime, the child or teen has to have somewhere to live. In this country, the child will go to live with foster parents. Foster parents are people who are paid by the government or agency to take care of children who cannot live with their birth parents. The child may have already been in several foster homes while the social worker was trying to help the birth parents improve their lives.

Children and teens who have been really badly harmed or neglected in their birth parent's home sometimes need treatment to get better. These kids go to treatment centers where there are doctors and counselors who provide help, so that the children can heal emotionally and learn better ways of managing behaviors.

Other children or teens sometimes go to group homes. These are also paid for by the government or agency to take care of kids, and these places usually have more children in them than a foster home. The group homes have paid staff who work shifts, and kids tend to arrive and leave more often than in foster homes.

In other countries, the child will go to live in an orphanage. In some orphanages, the adults take good care of the children and there is enough food and care for everyone. Some orphanages are not so good; the adults might not be kind, or there might not be enough food or clothing to go around. It can be a very lonely time for some children.

International Beginnings

In other countries, there might not be any judges involved because there are no child protection agencies like we have in this country. Instead, it is up to the birth parents to determine if they can raise their child. If the lives of the birth parents are so difficult and stressful that they realize they can no longer care for the child, they find an orphanage where their child will live and be cared for.

Sometimes the parents hope they can come back and get their child, but most of the time, they know that will never happen. Either they are too sick (they might have HIV or AIDS), or they live in a country where there is never going to be a way for them to earn a living and they know that their child would suffer and starve at home.

In some countries, parents find that they can keep the older children who can work and help the family survive, but they cannot afford to feed another baby or little child who can't contribute the family earnings. So, some of the children are kept in the family, and some are taken to the orphanage.

Up for Discussion: *The Details*

Questions you might want to discuss with your parents or your counselor. Some of them will apply to you, some won't. Just work on the ones that are right for your life:

- The names of the social workers who have helped in my adoption are...

- The names of all the people I have lived with...

- The names of all the towns and countries I have lived in...

- I was in foster care or an orphanage from the age of... till I was adopted at the age of...

- The names of the people who have taken care of me before I was adopted are...

Bekele's Story

Bekele, age eight, was adopted from Ethiopia and placed with a family in Canada. He lived in an orphanage from the time he was a baby until his adoptive parents went to Ethiopia and brought him home when he was four. He had some memories of his life in the orphanage, but they were pretty foggy. Mostly he remembered many other children and being outside a lot.

Bekele liked his new family right from the start. The parents were kind, and in his new family he had three teenage sisters who were always nice to him (as long as he stayed out of their bedrooms and didn't touch their stuff!). If he made them angry they would yell at him, but they never hit him.

Because Bekele didn't remember much about his life before he was adopted, he never knew what to say when people asked him about his adoption, or about where he came from. He still had some problems with the English language; it wasn't the same as he spoke when he was a little boy in Ethiopia but he couldn't remember the language he spoke when he lived there.

So, sometimes people would ask him questions that he could answer, but he couldn't find the words.

Bekele really hated it when people asked him why he had white parents and white sisters. He didn't have an answer for that question. He hated it when people asked him what happened to his African parents. He also hated it when people asked him about Ethiopia because he really didn't know anything about his birth country. His parents had taken him on a trip to Ethiopia the previous winter, but it was a lot of boring traveling and Bekele really would have much rather gone to Disneyland.

Most of the time Bekele just kept silent when people asked him about things he didn't understand. But sometimes he would feel angry because he didn't like that he didn't know any of the answers to his questions, and then he would yell at his parents or break something, even if it didn't belong to him. Sometimes he worried that he had been stolen from his first parents, or that his second parents had stolen him from the orphanage.

Bekele's Solution

What could Bekele do to fix this? What could Bekele's parents do to fix this? If you have these types of worries, here are some suggestions for you and your family to try:

- **Your parents can help you put together a Life Book with all the information they have about you and where you came from.** Your parents and your adoption worker can explain to you each step of your life that led up to your adoption, and who all the people were at each step.

- **Your parents can find out the names and positions of all the people who were involved in your adoption.** Include the workers or foster parents, the judges, the social workers and any other authorities in your Life Book. Even if you don't know their names, you should know what they did to help you get your family

- **Your parents can help you draw the story of everyone who was involved in your adoption.** It can begin like a train track with different stops along the way. Each stop represents a person who had something to do with your journey from your birthparents to your adoptive parents.

- **Your family can seek out other people from the same community, country or ethnic region that you came from.**

Bekele's family realized that he wasn't ready to deal with all that had happened in his past yet, but he needed a lot of help in dealing with his current life. He had had to make so many adjustments he just couldn't get his life going forward.

His parents had some people from the Ethiopian cultural center talk with them all about things Bekele had forgotten about "home" and so he had better answers when kids asked him questions. His parents also had his adoption worker come to the house and she drew out a diagram that showed all the people in his life from the time he went to the orphanage, until the time he was adopted. Bekele drew pictures of the people and wrote in their names (the ones he could remember) and that helped him have even more answers. He and his parents also rehearsed what he could say when kids or grown ups asked him about his life story, so he could chose whether to answer or not.

Bekele knew that someday he would need to have more information, but he knew that when that happened, he could ask his parents and they would help him find the answers. That was enough for now.

CHAPTER FOUR

What Kind of People Adopt Kids?

Once a child has been legally removed from the care of the birth parents, the social workers begin looking for a new family for that child. There are lots of people who want to parent children, and there are many reasons why people want to adopt.

Some of the main reasons adults adopt are:

They couldn't give birth to a child. Some adults can't get pregnant. When that happens to them, they know that they can still have a family by adopting a child who needs a family.

They didn't want to give birth to a child. There are adults who believe that there are already too many children in the world and they don't want to create more. Or, there may be some family history of genetic diseases and they don't want to risk making a child who would suffer with the disease. They would rather adopt a child who is already born and who needs parents.

They have given birth to children, but they would rather adopt the rest. The parents have had all the children they want through the birth process but they want more children, so they decide that the best way to increase their family is to adopt.

They feel called by God to adopt. People who have a strong religious faith may feel that they have been called by God to provide a loving family for a child who needs one.

They were adopted. People who have been adopted sometimes want to adopt a child because they know it was a good experience for them, and they want to offer that experience to another child.

They know people who have adopted. When people have friends or relatives who have adopted a child they see that it is a wonderful way to increase the family, and they decide to do the same.

They were fostering the child they have adopted. Foster parents don't usually start out planning to adopt because their job is to take care of the child until the child's new forever family is found. But some foster parents decide that they would like to become the permanent parents to a particular child, and so they adopt the child.

They responded to a recruitment campaign. Adoption agencies often seek out families by holding adoption events in churches or other public places. When the family saw the event ads, they realized that they would like to adopt.

They grew up in foster care and were never adopted. Adults who grew up without a family of their own sometimes want to provide a family to a child who doesn't have one.

They knew a child in foster care and decided to adopt him. Some people never thought about adopting but changed their minds after they met a particular child and decided that they would like to raise him.

Who Can Adopt?

Adults can't just walk into a foster home and pick a child to take home. They have to go through many steps to be approved as adoptive parents. First, they have to put in an application. On the application, they have to tell all kinds of personal things about themselves, and they also must write about what kind of child they would like to adopt. For example, they can state if they want only one child, or a sibling group, or if they want a child who is under five years of age, or if they would like to parent a teen.

After they have completed the application, they have to attend some courses on adoption. In these courses, they learn about things that happen with kids who have had a hard start in life, and they learn about kids who have Fetal Alcohol Spectrum Disorders (FASD), or Attention Deficit Hyperactivity Disorder (ADHD). These courses give them an understanding about the kinds of problems that kids may have, and they can begin thinking about how to help the child they will eventually adopt.

The adoptive parents also have to go through a home study. In order to do this, they have several meetings with a social worker who will come to their house and see what kind of place they live in, and what the community is like. The home study also asks prospective parents lots of questions about their child-rearing beliefs, how they earn a living, their religion and how they function in the world. Through the home study, the social worker tries to get to know the parents and to understand what they can offer a child. The social worker writes all of this information in a report so that other social workers can read it and decide if the family might be right for a child they have on their caseload.

Not all adoptive applicants are approved to adopt a child. Sometimes the home study will show that the adults who have applied don't have enough time or understanding of kids to be able to adopt successfully. Social workers may ask the applicants to take more courses on child development, or on parent-child communication, and then let them try again.

Some applicants are approved to adopt, but social workers never find a child who would fit well in their home so the applicants don't end up adopting.

Money

It costs a great deal of money to adopt a newborn baby. However, adopting a child who has been in foster care does not cost any money at the time of the adoption. It is not because the baby is more valuable than an older child; it's because newborn babies are usually placed for adoption with agencies that have to charge fees to cover the cost of the social workers and the paper work involved. Older kids who are in foster care or in residential treatment centers are usually placed by government departments or by agencies that are funded by the government. They have already been paid to do the homes studies and the adoptions, and they don't have to charge any extra fees to the adopting parents.

However, it costs a lot of money to raise a child, especially if the adoptive parents adopt a sibling group. The government people know that the adoptive parents may have to get a bigger house in order to have space for the child or children, and they know that one of the parents may have to quit work and stay home to raise the child. They also know that the child and the family may need counseling so that they can learn to live together and deal with any problems that may come up.

Most adoptive parents are not rich and could not afford to adopt a child if they had to pay for the bigger house, the time off work, the dental braces, and the counseling all by themselves. So, in many states and provinces, the government provides an amount of money so that the adoptive parents can afford to adopt. This is called an *adoption subsidy*.

This is not the same as being paid to raise the child. For one thing, it isn't ever a lot of money, but it is enough to allow more families to adopt than could afford to before this financial assistance was provided. Some adoptive parents don't get any money for their child or children, some decide they don't want the money, some don't need it. The rules about the adoption subsidy are different in every state and province, and the amount of money is different everywhere.

Up for Discussion: Your Adoptive Family

Here are some questions you might want to discuss with your parents or your counselor. Some of them will apply to you, some won't. Just work on the ones that are right for your life.

- Your parents decided to become adoptive parents because...

- Your parents decided to adopt you because...

- How long did your parents have to wait till they got to adopt you?

- Who else in your family is adopted?

- Did your parents have to go to adoption classes?

- Who else in the family was excited about your adoption?

Sierra's Story

Sierra, age thirteen, was adopted with her two older sisters when she was four, Charla was five and Olivia was eight. Her new parents already had two teenage sons when the girls came to live with them, but they were grown up and living away from home.

Sierra and Charla were pretty happy in their adoptive home right from the beginning, but Olivia could never fit in. She was mad at everyone all the time; the adoptive parents spent lots of time and energy trying to fix their relationship with Olivia, and to keep the family together.

There were a lot of counselors in their lives because Sierra and her sisters all had trouble learning in school, and since they had ADHD, their impulsiveness got in trouble at home and with their friends. But, their parents helped them and the tutors helped them and the special education teachers helped them, so everyone did okay...except Olivia.

One day, while Olivia and her mom were fighting, Olivia yelled at her mom and said "You're such a loser. Why did you want to adopt kids anyway? And who ever said you knew anything about being a mother?" Sierra heard her mom say "That question is just too silly to deserve an answer." Her sister's angry questions got Sierra thinking. Why *did* her parents adopt her and her sisters? They already had children, and Sierra had heard her dad say that they could have retired by now if they hadn't adopted more kids. Sierra wondered, who decides you can be a parent? When she went to bed that night, Sierra couldn't sleep. She kept thinking about those questions and wishing they weren't "too silly to deserve an answer" because even though she loved her parents and wasn't mad at them like Olivia, she was curious and wanted to know!

Sierra's Solution

What could Sierra do to fix this? What could Sierra's parents do to fix this? If you have these types of questions, here are some suggestions for you and your family to try:

- **Find a time when your parents aren't really busy and ask them why they wanted to adopt kids.** Ask your parents about what kinds of things they thought about when they applied to adopt.

- **Ask your parents if they took any courses about adoption.**

- **Ask your parents if they ever thought about adopting more kids.** What made them decide they had enough kids?

Sierra didn't feel comfortable asking her parents these types of questions, so she wrote them a letter and asked them to read it when they had time. In the letter, she asked them all the questions that were in the suggestions box. Sierra was really surprised to find out that her mom had always wanted to adopt children, and had hoped to adopt children even before she gave birth to her sons. Sierra's dad hadn't really thought about adoption when he was younger, but when they gave birth to two boys, he didn't want to add any more people to the world and he thought having daughters would be nice.

Sierra also found out that her parents took a lot of courses on adopting children from foster care so that they would be ready to deal with some of the problems that Olivia had. She was surprised when she realized that they adopted her and her sisters even though they knew that Olivia wouldn't adjust very well, and that they would have problems raising her. This made Sierra feel better because it meant that no matter what Olivia did, her parents would always love them all.

CHAPTER FIVE

Matching

Sometimes children or teens think that they were just placed in the first family that came along. That isn't the case. The decision about which child to place in which family is a complicated process called *matching*. This process happens in a variety of different ways, depending on the location and policies of the government or agency. Basically, matching is the social workers' attempts to match a child to a family that can best meet the child's needs. The matching isn't about looks; it's about interests, abilities, and beliefs.

Adoption has changed over the years. It used to be that the focus was on helping parents find a child. In the past, many adoptive families used to want a child who looked like they did, who was the same race, and who would fit into the family just like a birth child would have done. In those situations, the social workers would try to find a baby that matched the looks of the adoptive parents or who came from the same cultural background. People who still feel that way almost always adopt newborn babies. But over the years, social workers have realized that the best matches are the ones where the focus is not on finding the right child for a family, but on finding the right family for a child. They look first at what the child needs, and then they look for parents who can provide that care.

Also, people have changed what they think makes up a family, and most adoptive parents no longer believe that everyone has to look or think the same way in order to be a family. They are happy to have a child that is of a different race, or from another culture, or with special needs, or who is not going to 'fit' into the family like a birth child might have. They are prepared to love a child that can make his own place in the family, rather than replace a child who might have been born to them.

Social workers still consider some of the basic matching issues. For example, if they have a child who is Japanese, they might try to first find a family where one or both of the parents are Japanese. They do that to reduce how different a child might feel in the community in which the adoptive parents live. But, if they can't find the right kind of adoptive parents who are the same race as the child, then they will look for other qualities and characteristics that match. If the child likes sports, they will look for a family who is very athletic and likes to play sports. Or, if they have a child who loves the outdoors and animals, they will look for a family who lives on a farm.

Social workers also try to match kids with special needs with families with experience with those types of needs. For example, if a child has FASD, they might want to place him in a family that has already adopted kids with FASD because they know that the family understands the condition and knows how to get services for the child.

Older kids and teens who have thought about what they would like in a family may have requests that the social worker will try to match. The child might want a family who has lots of other kids, so the worker will look at the home studies of large families. Or, the teen might want a family who lives in a city, so the social worker will try to find home studies on adoptive parents who live in cities, rather than on farms.

Disappointment

Despite the best efforts of social workers, sometimes a child can't be matched to the type of family she wants. There may not be enough available families that match the child's criteria (or wish list) at that time. When that happens, the social workers look for other factors that match. They might try to find a family that laughs at the same kind of things the child laughs at, or they might try to find a family that lives in the same area as

41

birth relatives so that the child can visit, even if there are no other matching factors.

Sometimes, adoptive parents see a profile of a child on a photo listing on the computer, or in a book at their social worker's office. In these cases, the match has been made by the adoptive parents because there is something in the picture and the information about the child that tells them that they are the right family for that particular child. The social worker will still make the final decision about whether or not the child will go to that family, and even if the prospective adoptive parents want the child, they will not place the child in that home unless there are enough other matching factors.

Factors the social worker considers when trying to match a child to a family:

What is the adoptive parents' past history of commitment? The child's social worker wants to be sure that the adoptive parents know how to commit to a child. They don't want to place a child with someone who can't even keep a dog all of its life, or who has deserted children from a previous marriage, or who moves every year and changes jobs all the time. Everyone has to make changes in their lives sometimes, but people who make changes for no reason, or who make changes repeatedly, would not be a good match for a child who needs a stable family.

What does the couple want to get out of parenting? It's important to know *why* the couple or person wants to parent a child. If it is because they want to share their lives and their love with a child, that is a great match! If it is because they want to have someone to help them in their store, or to be a companion to their other children, or so they have someone to take care of them--that would be an awful match.

What is the couple's ability to relate to birth parents or past foster   parents? If the child has an existing relationship with his or her birth parents or foster parents, it's important to match the child with adoptive parents who will maintain that relationship and who can work out problems that might arise between the two families.

Do the prospective adoptive parents understand how much time the children will need from them? Is one parent able to stay home from work for a year or more? Do they have flexible work hours so that they can put their family first? When children come to a new family, everybody has to adjust and that takes time and energy. The social worker will try to match the child with a family who has the ability to be home with the child for awhile, so that everyone can get used to each other.

Is the environment / community / region going to meet the child's needs? Sometimes a child has special needs that require special services. When that happens, the social worker will try to find an adoptive family in an area where the services match the child's needs.

Social workers spend a great deal of time trying to match the child to the right family because they want the adoption to succeed. Some children spend a long time in foster care because the social worker is being very careful to find the right family, so that the child will never be rejected or moved again.

Up for Discussion: *Matching*

Questions you might want to think about...Some of them will apply to you, some won't. Just work on the ones that are right for your life:

- The adoption worker picked this family for me because...

- My parents knew I was the right child for them because...

- My parents proved to the worker they were the right parents for me by...

Marcus's Story

Marcus, age fourteen, had been waiting to be adopted since he was three years old. Some other kids in his foster homes had been adopted over the years, but no one had ever wanted to be his parents. Then one day, the adoption worker told him that he was going to be adopted by a couple from the other side of the country who were going to meet him next weekend. They would have some visits and if everything went well, they would take him home for good.

Marcus was stunned at the news. He had long ago given up any hope that he would find a family of his own, and now that it might happen, he wasn't too sure he was happy about it. He didn't mind moving again because he had already been in four different foster homes and he knew how to adapt. But he was kind of worried about what kind of people would pick a teenager to be their child. He was also kind of scared about what it would be like to live with them. Would they have anything in common? he wondered. He wanted to know what race they were, too, because so far he hadn't had foster parents who were the same race as he was. Maybe it didn't matter, but maybe it would; he wasn't sure.

Marcus was also worried about whether they would understand about his learning problems. He wasn't a bad kid, but he got in trouble at school when he was embarrassed about not being able to keep up with the other students in his class. He was also curious about whether these parents knew anything about skateboarding because that was his favorite pastime, and he didn't want to have to argue with them about hanging out at a skate park. It even occurred to him that maybe these people were perverts, because he just couldn't think who else would want him.

Marcus's Solution

What could Marcus do to fix this? What could Marcus' new parents do to fix this? If you have these kinds of thoughts, here are some suggestions for you and your family to try:

- **Before you're placed, ask the adoption worker why this family wants you.**

- **During the visits, ask the adoptive parents why they want you.**

- **As you get to know the family, ask them what they like to do with their time.** Do they have any hobbies? Will they will let you do the things you like doing now?

- **Ask the adoptive parents how they think you will all live together.** What do they think will change? How will they help you adjust? Who is going to help them adjust?

Marcus was smart; he made a list of all the questions he had about his new life and why these people wanted him. It turned out that Marcus's parents weren't the same race as he was, but they had three other adopted teenage sons who were, so he wouldn't be so different in this new home. He also found out that his soon-to-be adoptive parents had always wanted a large family; they had raised two of their boys since babyhood, and the third boy since he was seven. But, they felt that they didn't want to have little kids any more so when they decided to adopt one more time, they looked on the internet and saw Marcus's picture. They just knew he was meant to be their boy because two of their other sons loved skateboarding, just like Marcus.

Marcus still couldn't imagine what it would feel like to belong to a family of his own, but he had enough answers that he was now ready to give it a try.

CHAPTER SIX

Loss and Grief

Earlier in the book I mentioned that some kids think that when they get adopted they will not have any of the old problems that have challenged them for so long. But that's not the case, because even though the life around you changes when you are adopted, adoption doesn't change how you feel inside. You are still the same person. One of the things that *won't* change is your feelings of loss and grief for the people, places or things in your pre-adoption life. You may also find that you have even more loss when you have to leave your foster home, friends, school, and community, in order to be adopted.

Some kids who have had to deal with loss all of their lives have found ways to manage the feelings. Others think they have dealt with it, but have really only stuffed the feelings down deeper. And, for the kids who always thought they would eventually be able to live with their birth parents someday, adoption can really hurt because they have to face the fact that the loss of the birth parents is permanent.

Symptoms of Grief

Grief is a strange experience... sometimes a person can feel grief and not know what it is. For example, even though a child is happy to be adopted and likes his new adoptive parents, he might feel great sadness at leaving his foster parents and foster siblings, and maybe a pet dog or cat. The feelings get all jumbled up inside and make the child feel terrible, but he doesn't understand that the jumble is caused by grief.

Another odd and unpleasant thing about grief is that when a person feels grief over one loss, it leaks into all the other losses that have occurred in his life, and the feelings become even bigger. If a child is feeling loss over leaving his foster parents, the loss will leak into his original loss of his birth parents, and become a stronger feeling than he expected. It's as if there are all kinds of loss branches that lead into one big grief tree.

Symptoms of grief:

Difficulty concentrating. Grief can make it hard to think clearly. Sometimes children or teens appear to have attention problems when really they are grieving.

Apathy. A child might look like he doesn't care about anything, but it is only because he has learned to cope by not letting anyone know that he cares deeply.

Anger. When the grief is too much to cope with and it isn't recognized for what it is, the feelings can explode out in anger.

Guilt. The child is aware of feeling badly, but assumes that the negative feelings mean that he is bad or has done something wrong.

Eating and / or sleep disturbances. Grief can interrupt eating and sleeping patterns, especially when a child is transitioning to a new family where everything is different.

Irritability / mood swings. These are common symptoms of grief, but can be mistaken for a mood disorder in a child or teen.

Social withdrawal. Grief can make the child feel as if he doesn't want to be with other people or join into the activities of the new family.

Depression. Grief that is buried can cause depression. That means that the teen is always so sad that she can't cope with daily life and she doesn't have any interest in relationships with other people. She might sleep or eat too much or too little; she might stay away from people; she might even think about hurting herself or killing herself.

Emotional numbness. When feelings hurt too much, some kids learn to turn off all of their feelings. They can't feel the emotional pain, but they can't feel any good feelings either so they are emotionally cut off from people.

Feeling sad. This is a very normal part of grief. When a teen or child loses people or places or things he has cared about in his life, he can feel intense sadness for a long time.

Crying. Most people cry when they are grieving. It helps reduce the stress and tension from the loss, and is an important part of coping with loss.

Can't stop thinking or talking about the person, place or thing that is lost. A normal part of grief is to focus on what is gone. That is almost a way to hang on to it, or to the person. But, sooner or later, we have to let go, or else we won't make room in our lives for the good things and the good people who are still with us.

Resolving Grief and Loss

Grieving takes time. It can't be stuffed away and forgotten because it will just pop up again in some other way, such as a tantrum. The loss has to be acknowledged, talked about, and respected. There has to be time to heal from the loss--the process might take weeks, months, or even years.

For some kids, it will take a long time to get over the losses they've experienced in their lives. Then it becomes especially important to learn how to live with the losses and not let the grieving get in the way of the things that are still good in life. For example, some kids have a hard time getting over the loss of their birth parents. But, if they only think about the birth parents that couldn't raise them, then they won't learn to enjoy the adoptive families that they are living with now. The adoptive parents, the social workers, and a therapist can help a child or teen learn to move on from the grief and find a way to live with the losses without forgetting or being disloyal to the people who are no longer present in his or her life.

Instead of hanging onto the loss, it is best to acknowledge how much it hurt, do some really good, hard crying for a day, or even a week or a month, and then find a place in the memory where the lost people can live. Then you can move forward to get to know the new adoptive family and find out what all they have to offer.

Up for Discussion: *Grief and Loss*

Here are some things you might want to discuss with your parents or your counselor. Some of them will apply to you, some won't. Just work on the ones that are right for your life:

- I feel sad when I think about…

- The things that make other people feel sad make me feel…

- When I moved I had to leave some things behind. The things I miss the most are…

- I wish I could be with…

- I am afraid to feel happy when…

- The first time I remember being sad was when…

- The last time I cried was …

- When I miss someone from my past I …

- When I feel sad I …

Jaxon's Story

Jaxon, age ten, had been in foster care since he was four years old and during those years his mom had visited almost every month. He always liked the visits because his mom was so happy to see him, and told him how much she loved him. Jaxon knew that she couldn't take care of him because of her drug habit and because she never stopped her boyfriends from hurting him, but she always promised that she would go into treatment and get better. After every visit Jaxon hoped and prayed that this time her promises would be real.

Finally, the social worker told him that he was going to be adopted and then everything started to change really fast. Jaxon was happy that he was going to get a new family and live with parents who didn't take drugs and who had a clean house. Once he met them he was even happier. He loved the visits with his new family, and when he moved in with them, Jaxon couldn't believe how lucky he was. All kinds of wonderful things were happening! His new dad took him to skating lessons, and they watched hockey games and ate popcorn together on weekends. His new mom drove him to and from school every day, and she was a really good cook. The whole family went swimming together and to movies and they even let him have one of his new friends come for a sleepover.

Still, Jaxon felt confused. Sometimes his stomach or his head would hurt from the jumble of thoughts that went through his brain. He missed his birth mom a lot. Jaxon had taken care of his old mom when they still lived together, and he worried that now that he was adopted, she wouldn't even try to get into treatment. The adoption worker had explained that now that he had a new family, his old mother wouldn't be allowed to visit anymore. They were supposed to have one last visit, but his first mom hadn't shown up. The worker said she was probably too sad to say good bye. Jaxon knew that was true and it made him feel bad that he had hurt her by agreeing to the adoption. He worried that she would be mad at him if she knew how much he was beginning to like his new mom.

Jaxon didn't know what to do and the problem was beginning to make him angry. He didn't like feeling this way but he couldn't help it. And worse still, he had begun to get angry at his new parents and at school, and he was starting to worry that they wouldn't want to keep him if he didn't behave better.

Jaxon's Solution

What could Jaxon do to fix this? What could Jaxon's new parents do to fix this? If you have had these types of feelings, here are some suggestions for you and your family to try:

- **Find a way to tell your parents that you're feeling sad.** If you can't say the words, draw a picture of your sad self and show them. Ask your parents to help you with your feelings.

- **Tell your parents that you're worried about people from your past.** Tell your parents that you're scared that you have done a bad thing to your birth parents by being adopted.

- **Tell your parents that you feel confused about being adopted.** Let your adoptive parents take care of you.

Jaxon didn't tell his parents what he was feeling, but they could see that something was wrong so they took him to a counselor who figured it out. She did a lot of things to help him learn to talk to his adoptive parents about his fears and worries, and about how sad he sometimes felt. She also helped his adoptive parents learn to listen better when he was sad and helped them understand what they could do to comfort him.

Jaxon also had to learn that some of his sadness would never go away, but he didn't have to let sad feelings wreck his good new life. Now, when Jaxon feels sad or worried, he draws his feelings on a paper and shows his parents, or sometimes he keeps the drawing to himself and puts it in a scrap book his parents got him. Jaxon has also learned to ask his parents for a cuddle or a hug when he's sad, and he's learning that he isn't responsible for taking care of his birth mom. Jaxon knows he will have sad feelings all his life, but he isn't afraid anymore to let the happy feelings happen too.

CHAPTER 7

Forming a Family Identity

Now that you have moved into your new home, the whole family will have to transform into something it wasn't before. That's right, *everyone* has to change! This can be very difficult for the whole family. It's a time of adjustment where every member of the family finds out about each other and learns how to live together. Some people think that just because a child or teen has lived with other families before being adopted, that he knows how to adapt to any family he moves in with. But in fact, when a person gets adopted it's just the opposite. That's because when a child lived with the previous foster families, he didn't have to become part of that family. The child didn't have to become anyone's son; he just had to live there and try to get along. The foster parents and the child all know that sooner or later the child will be moving, so there is no attempt to change anyone.

But when you get adopted it is very different. The adoptive parents really want the child or teen to become *theirs*. They aren't just worried about whether the kid behaves; they worry about how well he is doing in school, and whether he will go to college, and what kind of friends he is hanging out with – or even if he has friends. They want to bring all kinds of wonderful things in to their new child's life, and even though that is well intentioned, it can feel like a lot of pressure on a kid.

The adopting parents are also going through a lot of changes. They may never have been parents before so they have to learn all kinds of new things. And if they are already parents, they still have to learn how to be parents to their newest child. It can often seem to children and teens that parents should know how to be parents before they have kids, but in fact, being a parent is a learning process that never ends. When a new child enters the family, everyone has to work together to create a new family identity.

Challenges in building a new family identity:

The child or teen has divided loyalties. The child or teen might feel that in order to be loyal to past foster parents or to birth parents, he can't let himself feel good about being part of a new family. Adopted children may worry that if they learn to love the new mom and dad, they will lose, or hurt, people from their past.

The child believes he was stolen from his birth family, and can't accept that he has new parents. Many children are removed from their birth families at a time of crisis. Sometimes the police arrive in the middle of the night to take the child because other people have alerted the child protection workers that the parents are too drunk, too stoned or too violent to take care of the child. The parents may have cried and the child may have tried to hang onto the parents because he or she didn't understand what was happening. The child may have been afraid of being taken away to live with strangers. This makes the child feel like he was stolen even though he wasn't.

Self-protection. The child or teen is afraid to feel love for the new parents because he or she has been let down or abandoned by so many parents before. They don't trust that these new parents won't leave just like everyone else has.

Living like a boarder. Some kids get along in the different homes and different families by living as if they were a boarder--someone who just pays rent but doesn't really belong to the family. In some ways that was previously true, because the child didn't belong to the foster families, and the foster families were paid to have him.

Feeling un-entitled. Some kids feel that they are not good enough for the adopting parents or the new family. They may feel that things they have done in the past make them too 'bad' for the parents, or they may feel that bad things that have been done to them mean they don't deserve to be loved by such good people.

High expectations. Some adopting parents have expectations that are too hard for the child to handle. Adopting parents want the best for their new child, but they don't have any way of knowing what the child can or can't do. They may ask the child to behave better, or to learn more quickly, when it is too soon for the child to be able to do so.

Even though it may seem like you will never feel part of this new family, you will find that eventually you fit in, and the family has changed to include you as if you had always been there. It's very important that the entire family, including the new parents and you, give this whole situation some time to work itself out. If everyone tries to rush how they feel about each other, and if everyone tries to pretend that nothing has changed, then it well take a long, long time before you really begin to feel like you are part of this family.

Most people find that it takes at least a year and a half before all family members feel like the changes are normal. I know that seems like a long time, but there are still lots of good things that can be happening in the meantime. You can still practice calling the new parents "mom" and "dad", even if it doesn't feel right yet. And, you can start making friends in your new community and learning what good things your new school has to offer. Even if you aren't sure if you like your new dad, you'll find that you can use the time you have with him (when he takes you to soccer practice or swimming lessons, for example) to get to know him, and to let him get to know you. After all, you can't love a stranger, so the more you tell your new parents about yourself, and the more you ask about them, the more you will find that you all have in common.

It's very important that you use the first few months in the new home to find out what the adoptive parents think and believe about life and about the world. Are they religious? If so, you can ask them how they came to have their faith and you can talk to them about your feelings about God and religion. You might not have the same beliefs, but you can at least learn to understand and respect what is different and enjoy what is the same. You can also ask your adoptive parents what they hope your life will be like now that you are their child. And, you can tell them the kind of things you want to get out of your growing up years in their home. I know this can sound kind of scary and complicated, but if you go slowly, it will be easier.

Family Meetings

One way to have these conversations is to have family meetings. You can ask your adoptive parents if you can all meet together once a week to talk about things that are important to each of you, and to ask each other questions so that you can get to know each other better. Some of the questions you are asked might feel too private and you don't want to answer them. That's okay, you just have to politely tell the asker that you aren't ready to talk about that issue yet. And you might find that some of the questions you ask aren't going to be answered for the same reason. Again, just say "okay" and move on. Everyone has the right to privacy, but people will usually tell each other quite a bit about themselves if they understand that the other person really wants to get to know them better, and is not just being nosey.

You might find that the adoptive parents like to do things that you haven't done before. For example they might like to ski or skate, and you come from a place where nobody did either of those sports. Don't be afraid to try the new activities. You might be surprised at how much you like some of them, or how good you can become! Just because you haven't done an activity before is no reason not to start now. There are lots of ways of enjoying life and having fun, and you want to be open to learning new ways to spend fun time with your family, and to be happy.

Up for Discussion: *Adjusting*

Here are some things you might want to discuss with your parents or your counselor. Some of them will apply to you, some won't. Just work on the ones that are right for your life:

- The hardest thing to get used to in my new family was...

- The biggest change after the adoption was...

- The easiest thing to get used to in my new family was...

- I expected...

- I didn't expect...

- I'm still uncomfortable with...

- The best surprise in my new family was...

- I have contributed....to my new family.

- My new family has helped me to...

Joelle's Story

Joelle, age twelve, was really happy to finally get a family. Her birth mom had dropped out of her life when she was very young and she never knew her birth dad. Joelle had been in a four different foster homes. They were all nice people, but for some reason she had been moved from each of them after just a couple of years. Joelle had waited to be part of a family for a long time and had almost given up when the social worker finally said that someone actually wanted to adopt her.

Joelle really enjoyed the pre-placement visits and everything went well right from the start. The parents had two other adopted children, a boy, age eighteen, and a girl, age seventeen, who were really busy with their own lives but who were nice enough when they were around. The parents took Joelle shopping; they let her pick out her own bedding and helped paint her new bedroom the color she wanted.

Joelle was really happy when she finally moved in. But, after Joelle had been in the home a few months, she started to feel like maybe it wasn't going to be as good as she first thought.

Joelle felt that her new parents really invaded her privacy. They checked her homework every day and made sure she did it all. When she failed math, they put her in afterschool tutoring, and reduced her computer time till she could bring up her grades. Joelle didn't like that; she had always done okay in school but these parents seemed to want her to get way higher grades than she had ever achieved before. They kept saying she was a smart girl and should do better in school so that she could go to college when she was older. Joelle didn't see any reason to do better; she had never thought about going to college before, and wasn't interested now.

Her new parents were also picky about her clothes and make up. She had liked it at first when they bought her all new clothes, but then she realized that they had kind of tricked her into getting rid of her old outfits. They wouldn't let her wear make up until she was fourteen. All her life, social workers and counselors had been telling her that it was her body and only she could decide what was to be done with it, and now these parents were telling her every day that some item of clothing "wasn't appropriate" or that she couldn't wear eye liner to church.

Plus, there were the stupid rules about friends. The parents had to meet everyone she wanted to hang out with. Joelle had to bring her friends home so the parents could get to know them, and the parents wouldn't let her go anywhere unless they knew who she was going to be with and where she was going to be.

Joelle tried to talk with her new older sibs about these rules, but they weren't any help at all. They told her that they hadn't always liked the rules when they were younger, but the rules were for her own good and she'd understand that when she got older. Well, that just made Joelle madder and more frustrated, and also showed her that she didn't have any friends in her new house.

The worst thing? Her new family did too many things together. Joelle liked to use her free time to go to malls and just hang out, but her parents made her get up early every Sunday to go to church. They also made her go with them when they volunteered as a family to work at the local animal shelter. On special occasions like Thanksgiving and Christmas, the family volunteered to help feed street people and she had to go along, too! Her new brother and sister participated in these events and acted like they were having fun. They said it was important to give back to the community because they had a lot and other people didn't have as much. Joelle had never been selfish but she hadn't had much in her own life till she got adopted, and she didn't see why she now had to hang around sad animals and sick adults.

Joelle knew that parents had the right to tell kids how to live, but she wasn't really their kid. She didn't belong to these people with their weird ideas, and she wasn't sure she wanted to. The adoption hadn't been finalized yet, and it was getting to the point where Joelle was going to tell the social worker that she wanted to go back to foster care.

Joelle's Solution

What could Joelle do to fix this? What could Joelle's new parents do to fix this? If you have ever felt this way, here are some suggestions for you and your family to try:

- **Make a list of all the things that you have in common with your new parents.** For example, do you have the same color hair as anyone else in the family? Do you and someone else in the family both like music or reading?

- **Try to do some new things with your new parents.** Your new parents will have lots of activities that they like to do and you can try to do some of them to see which you like. They can also try some of the things you like, too, so invite them to join in some activities that you like.

- **Know that just because you joined a new family, it doesn't mean you are a new person.** Everybody in your new family is an individual, just as you are. Getting adopted means *adding* to your life, not changing the basics of 'you'.

- **Give yourself time.** You can't expect to feel part of this new family right away. You might feel like a guest for a while, or you might feel like you're still a foster child in another temporary home. Don't worry, these feelings are perfectly natural and they will go away with time.

- **Your family can attend adoptive family events with other families that are like yours.** It can be really helpful to be other families that are like yours and you can see how other kids have adjusted to their new lives.

- **Ask questions.** Ask your new parents about themselves. Ask to see pictures of their lives when they were kids so that you can get a sense of who these people are.

- **Talk to your parents or someone about the things you feeling about your new family that are confusing or that you don't like.** Your new parents can't change their whole lives around, but they will probably be willing to change some things because they want you to be happy and to feel like you belong.

Joelle was getting more and more frustrated but she didn't want to talk to her new parents about her feelings, and she didn't like the counselor they took her to visit. One day she went to the movies with her new older sister and on the drive home she found herself talking about all of the things that were making her so mad. This time, her sister really listened to her, and when they got home, her sister had her tell the parents about her feelings.

Much to Joelle's surprise, the parents were actually interested in hearing what she had to say and they agreed that maybe they could compromise on some of the issues. Joelle's mom even said that she thought maybe they had tried to make too many changes in Joelle's life too soon, so they talked about what each of them could live with and what they couldn't. For example, they finally understood that Joelle hated going to feed the hungry adults, so they agreed to let her hang out with her new grandparents while the rest of the family volunteered. They also agreed that they didn't have to meet all of her friends, just the ones she was spending most of her time with.

Joelle didn't get as much changed as she would have liked, but even that little bit made her feel more appreciated for who she was instead of feeling like the new parents were trying to turn her into someone else. In return, she quit complaining about not being allowed to wear eye make up to church.

Two and half years after the adoption, Joelle really started to feel like she belonged with this family, and they seemed to like her for who she was.

CHAPTER 8

Attachment

Attachment is a word that is used over and over again in adoption. The biggest concern of all the adults in your life is whether or not you can *attach* to your adoptive parents. They worry about this because attaching to parents is how you learn to have healthy relationships with all the other people who will ever be in your life when you are an adult. It is how you learn to care about and get along with other people, how you learn to be a good person, and how to grow up to someday be a good parent.

How Did You Get Attachment Challenges?

Children develop attachment problems when

- they have multiple caregivers, such as having more than one or two foster homes, or are shuffled from one relative to another

- when the original parents' style of parenting is not very good, or is inconsistent, or violent

When these things happen in your life, your brain becomes focused on helping you, as a baby or little child, to develop skills that will help you *survive* instead of *developing skills that will help you have healthy and loving relationships.*

For some children, this means that they only know how to get what they need to survive by manipulation, control, aggression, or by withdrawal. The infant grows into childhood with a strong sense of abandonment, but no understanding at all of how to belong to or trust a parent figure. This might be how you have learned to survive in the world, or it might not. All children and youth are different.

Some people consider attachment disorder to be a behavioral problem, which means that they expect the child to be able to change his behavior by choice, or simply by learning more acceptable ways of behaving. Some adoptive parents believe that once their newly placed child has a stable and safe family life, he will immediately be able to love them and behave for them as if he had always been a part of their family. Some kids believe the same thing, but that isn't the way it works. Developing attachment takes time and your parents will have to learn new skills to help you to do this.

The good news is that attachment problems can be fixed. And, since you have been adopted, you are now in the right place with the right people because attachment problems are fixed when your brain changes. You brain can begin to change now that you are in a stable, permanent family and are living with people who want to love you, and who want to be your parents forever

Attachment problems aren't the same for everyone. Your brain might have the   ability to attach, but you never had anyone with whom you could develop a healthy attachment-based relationship. Or, you may have the ability to attach to siblings, but again, you have lacked a permanent, stable, loving parent to stretch your love over to and include. It can be helpful to think of yourself as being in a pre-attachment stage, which will be followed by an early attachment, when you begin to develop some sense of stability. This is followed by a more fully developed attachment which includes loyalty, sharing good and bad feelings in a healthy way, and feeling trust in the people who love you.

None of this means you are weird. It's just what happens to kids who don't begin life with stable parents or who have too many different people taking care of them. You will be fine and your brain will be just like everyone else's. You just have to give it time with your new parents.

Characteristics of an Attachment Challenge

Every child is different, so each child will show his level of attachment, or lack of attachment, in slightly different ways. Children and youth who have attachment challenges display many different types of behaviors. These behaviors and reactions begin when a child is very young, and are reactions to the relationships a child has with his or her parents or caretakers.

When your parents or your therapist talk about attachment problems with you, it's important to look at the overall picture. It's very important to remember that these challenges don't mean you are a bad person, or a mean or unlovable person. There are many good things about you, and you might want stop *right now* and make a list of your positive traits so you don't forget!

Children with attachment challenges may display a few, or many, of the following behaviors:

Destructive Behavior. Children might damage or break toys or objects that belong to the adoptive parents, teachers, or neighbors, and may not even feel sorry about it later. Some kids will claim the damage was an accident, while other children will be honest and admit that they have purposely broken the object-- but they can't understand why everyone is so mad about it.

Unfeeling Behavior. It may be hard for kids to understand that hugs are an emotional experience that is *shared between two people*, not something that is used for manipulation or trade purposes: "I'll hug mom now so that she will let me watch the television later". Some kids may cruelly tease or taunt less powerful children, hurt animals, argue about everything and boss other kids, because they can't understand what this behavior feels like for the other person; they are unable to participate in a healthy relationship. A very few children will act out serious crimes with intent to harm, and will never feel a sense of remorse.

Charming Behavior. Charm is displayed at will, but generally only when the child is interacting with someone they rarely see, or will never see again. For example, they can be very charming and delightful to strangers, therapists, store keepers, and even visiting adoptive grandparents, but these children act very differently toward their adoptive parents.

Controlling Behavior. Some kids or teens try to get what they want by *forcing* their will by manipulation, aggression or withdrawal. As little kids, their brains were too busy focusing on survival to develop the parts that normally deal with positive interaction; these kids use 'control' because they don't trust anyone to actually give them what they want or need. Food and sleep may become control battlegrounds: children may under-sleep or over-sleep (whichever works worst for the family schedule!), and food may be stolen, avoided or hoarded-- as long as the child feels in *control* of it.

Anxious Behavior. The child or teen may demand attention by yelling, hitting or throwing objects, or, he or she may cling anxiously to a parent like a barnacle, even trying to follow mom or dad into the bathroom!

Impulsive Behavior. Children with low impulse control have a high level of energy, almost like Attention Deficit Disorder (ADD). These kids will make quick choices before thinking about consequences, or before thinking about how others might feel about their behavior.

Devious Behavior. Some kids will steal items they want, or even items that don't interest them at all; some children lie when there is no apparent need to do so.

Affectionate Behavior. Children might find it easier to be *inappropriately* affectionate with total strangers. They might not be hugging the mail carrier, but they might find it way easier to be nice to teachers or grandparents than it is to be nice to their new parents.

Intimate Behavior. Looking in another person's eyes for any length of time can be a difficult and uncomfortable degree of contact for some adopted children. Eye contact skills are supposed to develop in early infancy and this is very important to brain development. For most children who have attachment problems, there was no safe adult to look deeply into their eyes in those early days.

Solitary Behavior. Hurt children may have learned how to ignore pain and fear and rarely allow someone else to comfort them. They know how to take care of themselves, but they have no clue how to let others take care of them--they do not even understand that 'caring' is what the adoptive parent is trying to do.

What are all of these behaviors and characteristics really about? Children with attachment challenges never had a loving, safe adult to take care of their feelings. This means they haven't yet learned how to trust other people to take care of them, and they haven't learned how to care about the feelings of other people.

Your adoptive parents will try to help you get over this emotional hurdle. Learning to trust your new parents and learning to care about your relationships with other people will make you feel much better. There are many things your parents and therapist can do to nurture attachment that are effective and helpful, but remember, change takes time!

Up for Discussion: *Healthy Attachment*

Here are some things you might want to discuss with your parents or your counselor. Some of them will apply to you, some won't. Just work on the ones that are right for your life:

- Why does it matter if I "attach" or not?

- How will I know if I become attached?

- Will I have to change a lot to be attached?

- Will my parents keep me even if I never attach to them?

Steven's Story

Steven was almost seven when he was adopted. He couldn't remember his birth parents and he couldn't remember most of the eight foster parents he had lived with. He had been with the last foster parents for a few years but he always felt like they liked the other kids in the house better than him. One day, his social worker told him he was going to be adopted into a large family. There were four other brothers and three sisters already in the home. That was quite a surprise to Steven and he wasn't sure he would like to live with so many people, but he knew he didn't have a choice.

It turned out that Steven didn't mind the new family too much. There were lots of toys and there was always someone to play with. But, the other kids seemed to manage a lot better than he did... they were always getting him in trouble just because he lied about taking or breaking their toys. When Steven was caught, the new parents always got mad at him and put him in time-out at the kitchen table. Steven was in trouble with the parents a lot too; they accused him of stealing food and lying. The worst thing was, his parents were always after him to admit what he did, even when he couldn't remember doing it!

The new parents went ahead with the adoption and everyone told Steven he would grow up in this family. The funny thing was, having Steven grow up in his new family seemed more important to everyone else than it did to Steven. He didn't really care if he stayed or not.

Steven's Solution

What could Steven do to fix this? What could Steven's new parents do to fix this? If you have ever felt this way, here are some suggestions for you and your family to try:

- **Let your new parents touch you by holding your hand or with a nice hug.** Your mom can help you shampoo your hair in the sink, or your parents can rub your back or your arms. If you are comfortable with being hugged, try to initiate some family hugs once in a while.

- **Sing with your parents.** I know that sounds weird, but singing with other people can make you feel more connected with them. Of course, you'll have to find some music that you can all agree on first!

- **Play with your parents.** You can all go skating or swimming or cycling or skiing together. It's really good to get outside with them and use up your energy together. You can also play board games and go to movies or concerts together. You might try cooking or baking as a family.

- **Don't try to trust the new parents too soon.** In an adoption, everyone thinks that the parents and kids should all trust each other right away. But that never really works. Instead, take the pressure off yourself and let the experiences you share with them be the foundation for learning to trust over time.

- **Don't look for their faults.** It's really easy to find faults in other people. But if you want to learn to love them, then you need to be looking for the good things about the new parents. Are they kind to animals? Do they listen to you when you speak to them? Do they make you laugh sometimes?

- **Forgive the new parents when they do things 'wrong'.** Your new parents will do their best to do everything right for you, but they can't possible be perfect. They'll make mistakes. Sometimes they'll be too strict, and sometimes they'll be too easy. And sometimes they just won't understand. But that's part of being human.

- **Try to relax.** Getting adopted is a lot of work and takes up a lot of mental energy. Try to just relax sometimes, and let go of trying to hold your world together. Your new parents can control the family well enough, so practice letting go of controlling everything around you.

- **Try to look them in the eye when they talk to you.** Eye contact is very important in human relationships and it's a big part of establishing attachment. You may not be used to looking directly into people's eyes, but this is a good time to start trying. Just do a little bit at a time and expand how long you can maintain eye contact, until you can do it for a whole conversation.

- **Talk to your new parents.** You have a million feelings, thoughts and ideas, but your new parents can't read your mind to find out what those things are. Help them get to know you by telling them about yourself, and what you think and feel. If you don't like some of the new rules and expectations have a conversation about how you feel.

- **Listen to your new parents and new siblings.** Your new family members are just like you; they have thoughts and feelings and ideas too, so *talk* to them and *ask* your new family members questions about themselves. For example, ask them where they grew up, or what they did or didn't like about school when they were your age. If you bring up the issue of rules or expectations that you don't like – be prepared to *listen* to their reasons for the rules.

- **Go to counseling.** You may need help learning to talk with your parents and learning to listen to them. A counselor can help your family learn how to effectively connect.

- **Don't expect miracles.** You and your parents are all trying to learn how to live together and how to love each other. This won't happen overnight. You have a long history of people leaving you and lying to you, and it will take a while before you heal from past experience. Don't get mad at your parents just because they can't make it better right away. Give them, and yourself, credit for trying.

Steven's parents knew that it would take him a long time to *attach* to them, so they kept telling him that even though he was in trouble a lot, they still loved him and life would get better. Steven didn't really understand what that meant, but even though he waited to be moved, one day he realized he'd been in his new family for three years and no one had moved him yet. He also realized that he wasn't in as much trouble as he used to be. He started to admit to his behaviors most of the time, and he didn't lie or steal quite as much. He also had learned to hug his parents and that felt kind of good. When Steven went to sleep at night he didn't have bad dreams anymore, at least not often, and when he did, he now trusted that if he called out, his mom or dad would come to his room and cuddle him until he felt better.

In fact, by the time Steven was nine years old, he was starting to think that maybe he *did* want to stay in this family, and to believe that maybe he really would grow up with them.

Conclusion

Growing up is difficult and challenging and the whole point of *parents* is having people in your life who will guide you and love you and take care of you. When life feels hard, parents will help you and teach you how to manage. Once you are adopted, you have the chance to learn to really love someone who isn't going to hurt you, leave you or make you take care of yourself.

Many kids who are adopted feel overwhelmed at first. Many parents who adopt feel the same way. It's not easy to learn to be a family together, and for everyone to change and adapt to each other and to the new joys and challenges you've all brought into the other's lives. But, life is about change, and you must know that by now since you have likely had way too many changes in your life already!

Adoption, while it's one massive change all at once, will lessen how often you have to make changes in the long run, and it will give you the opportunity to grow up without worrying about adult problems. You can be a kid, have friends, have fun, and have support and help to work out the problems that come your way.

You deserve a family of your own, and now you have one...work with your new parents to make your family the best it can be!